Masterpiece

Comprehension
LOWER JUNIOR
Helena Rigby

Contents

Name _____   Date _____

Diagnostic assessment – Poetry

The scarecrow

He stands upon his single leg,
His body stuffed with hay,
And holds his gloved hands wide apart
To scare the birds away.

A battered hat upon his head,
A carrot for a nose,
He might fool me, he might fool you –
But he doesn't fool the crows.

by John Yeoman

1   What does the scarecrow wear on his hands?

_____   **Set A**

2   What is used for his nose? _____   pages
3   On the back of this sheet, draw and colour a picture of the   3 - 4
    scarecrow.

4   What is the scarecrow supposed to be doing?

_____

5   Why do you think the scarecrow would need to do this?   **Set B**

_____   pages
                                                          5 - 6
6   List the things you would need to make a scarecrow like this.

_____

7   In what places could you find a scarecrow?

_____

8   How would he hope to 'fool the crows'?   **Set C**

_____   pages
                                                          7 - 8
9   Do you think he could fool you or me? Why?

_____

Name _____ Date _____

Five little monkeys

The verses of this poem are in the wrong order!

A One little monkey cried all afternoon,
   So they put him in an aeroplane
   And sent him to the moon.

B Four little monkeys climbed up a tree;
   One of them tumbled down,
   Then there were three.

C Two little monkeys found a currant bun;
   One ran away with it;
   Then there was one.

D Five little monkeys walked along the shore;
   One went a-sailing,
   Then there were four.

E Three little monkeys found a pot of glue;
   One got stuck in it,
   Then there were two.

   Anon

1 Write the letters in the order you think the verses should be.

_____

2 Write the sentence that is true.
   The five little monkeys were shopping.
   The five little monkeys were at the seaside.

_____

3 Choose one of the verses, and draw a picture of it.
   Write the verse underneath your picture.

Name _____ Date _____

The alien

The alien
Was as round as the moon.
Five legs he had
And his ears played a tune.
His hair was pink
And his knees were green,
He was the funniest thing I'd seen.
As he danced in the door
Of his strange spacecraft,
He looked at me –
And laughed and laughed!

by Julie Holder

Answer these questions in sentences.

1   What shape was the alien?

_____

2   How many legs did the alien have?

_____

3   What could the alien do with his ears?

_____

4   How can you tell the alien came from space?

_____

5   Why do you think the alien was laughing?

_____

Turn over and draw and colour a picture of the alien and his spacecraft.

Name _____ Date _____

If you should meet a crocodile

The verses of this poem are in the wrong order!

A   Whene'er you meet a crocodile
       He's ready for his dinner.

B   Ignore the welcome in his smile
       Be careful not to stroke him.

C   If you should meet a crocodile
       Don't take a stick and poke him;

D   For as he sleeps upon the Nile
       He thinner gets and thinner;

Anon

1   Write the letters in the order you think the verses should be.

_____

2   What do you think the crocodile might do if you stroked him or
    poked him with a stick?

_____

3   Where do you think the crocodile in the poem is?

_____

4   Draw and colour a picture to illustrate the poem.

Name _____ Date _____

A watering rhyme

Early in the morning,
Or the evening hour,
Are the times to water
Every kind of flower.
Watering at noonday
When the sun is high,
Doesn't help the flowers,
Only makes them die.

Also, when you water,
Water at the roots;
Flowers keep their mouths where
We should wear our boots.
Soak the earth around them,
Then through all the heat
The flowers will have water
For their thirsty 'feet'!

by P.A. Ropes

Answer these questions in sentences.

1   When are the best times to water flowers?

_____

2   What time of the day is noon?

_____

3   What happens if the flowers are watered when the sun is high?

_____

4   What should the ground be soaked with?

_____

5   What part of the flower drinks the water?

_____

6   At what time of the year would this poem be most useful?

_____

Name _____ Date _____

Gruesome

The verses of this poem are in the wrong order!

A Cautiously I opened it
and there to my surprise
a little GRUE lay sitting
with tears in its eyes.

B 'Exercises are the answer,
each morning you must DO SOME.'
He thanked me, smiled,
and do you know what?
the very next day he ...

C I was sitting in the sitting room
toying with some toys
when from the door marked: 'GRUESOME'
there came a GRUESOME noise.

D 'Oh little GRUE please tell me
what is it ails thee so?'
'Well I'm so small,' he sobbed,
'GRUESSES don't want to know'.

by Roger McGough

Answer these questions in sentences.

1   Write down the letters in the order you think the verses should be.

_____

2   Describe what you think a Grue might look like.

_____

_____

3   Complete the last line of the poem. Think carefully about the spelling.

_____

Name _____ Date _____

Five eyes

In Hans' old mill his three black cats
Watch his bins for the thieving rats.
Whisker and claw, they crouch in the night
Their five eyes smouldering green and bright;
Squeaks from the flour sacks, squeaks from where
The cold wind stirs on the empty stair,
Squeaking and scampering, everywhere.
Then down they pounce, now in, now out,
At whisking tail, and sniffing snout;
While lean old Hans he snores away
Till peep of light at break of day;
Then up he climbs to his creaking mill,
Out come his cats all grey with meal –
Jekkel, and Jessup, and one-eyed Jill. .

by Walter de la Mare

Answer these questions in sentences.

1   Where do the three black cats live?

_____

2   Why does Hans keep the cats?

_____

3   Who is asleep while the cats are awake?

_____

4   Why is the poem called 'Five eyes'? Do you think this is a good title?

_____

5   What was kept in the bins?

_____

6   What do you think had happened once to the cat called Jill?

_____

Diagnostic assessment – Letters

4th July

**Sandmarsh First School,
Sandmarsh, Wrecking,
WG1D 4BR**

Dear Parent,

The school is holding a jumble sale on the last Saturday of the term.
We hope to buy a colour printer for our new computer with the money we
raise. It will help the children with their reading and writing.

   The jumble sale will start at 2 o'clock. We would be very pleased if
you could give us any good clothes, books and toys that you and your
family have finished with. Articles for a White Elephant stall would be
welcome. Jumble can be left at the school on the Friday before the sale.

   We also need extra helpers for making refreshments. Please let me know
if you can help.

Yours sincerely,

Eva Boot
Headteacher

---

1 Where is the jumble sale being held?
_____

2 What will the money be used for?
_____

3 What does the school need for the jumble sale?
_____

Set A
pages 10 - 11

---

4 Who is giving all the things for the jumble sale?
_____

5 Does the school want worn-out clothes?
_____

6 What are the parents being asked to help with?
_____

Set B
pages 12 - 13

---

7 In which term is the jumble sale to be held?
_____

8 What might you find on a White Elephant stall?
_____

9 What is the age range of the children at the school?
_____

Set C
pages 14 - 15

Name _____ Date _____

Thank you

> 8 West Street,
> Aston,
> AN5 4BY
>
> 9th April
>
> Dear Aunty Jill,
> Thank ____ very much for the lovely paint box you ____ me.
> I was saving ____ to buy one so I was very ____ that I had
> one for my birthday.
> Rani gave ____ a painting book and I have already coloured
> two pictures. I ____ sending you a picture of your house.
> I painted ____ myself. I hope you ____ it.
> Love
> Joshua

1   Write the missing words in the letter.

| you   am   pleased   gave   like   it   up   me |

Answer these questions in sentences.

2   Who is Joshua's letter for?

_____

3   Why is Joshua writing the letter?

_____

4   What did Rani give to Joshua?

_____

5   What did Joshua send to Aunty Jill?

_____

6   Why was Joshua pleased with the paint box?

_____

Name _____ Date _____

Party

9 Cliff Road
Dunwick
SA7 3ND

4th September

Dear Lucy,

I am having my birthday party on Saturday 6 September.
I hope you can come. We are going to the Leisure Centre
for a swimming party. After swimming we are coming back
to my house. Dad says he will do a barbecue for us!
Mum is going to do a treasure hunt in the garden.

Come round to my house at 3 o'clock. Aunty Vicky and
Mum will take us to the Leisure Centre. Don't forget
your swimming things! The party will end at 7 o'clock
but Mum says you can sleep over if you want. Please
let me know if you can come.
                Love
                    Helen

Complete these sentences by writing in the missing words.

1   Helen asked _____ to her birthday party.

2   The party starts at _____ .

3   Afterwards in the garden there will be a _____ and a
    _____ _____ .

4   The weather will need to be _____ for playing in the
    garden.

5   If Lucy wants to stay the night she must bring her _____ .

Invitation

5 Park Street,
Croft,
WN7 1 0EP
21st August

Dear Ashi

How _____ you? I am having a _____ time at Gran's house. My cousins, Mark and Kevin have _____ round to play. They live in the next street so _____ can come on their bikes.
   We all went to the _____ side on Monday. I took my new kite. Kevin fell over when he was running with my _____ to get it to fly. He flattened a little girl's sand castle. She ____ such a loud noise crying she woke up her Dad. He shouted at Kevin and we ran _____ to Gran.
   I am coming home on Saturday at dinner _____. Come round to play in the afternoon and _____ for tea. I will show you my holiday photographs. I have got a present for you.

Love,
   Emma

1   Write the missing words in the letter.

| kite | are | stay | made | good | come | back | sea | they | time |

Answer these questions in sentences.

2   Why is Emma writing a letter?

_____

3   Who are Mark and Kevin?

_____

4   What was the weather like on the beach?

_____

5   Why is Emma going home on Saturday?

_____

Complaint

Choccy Chocolates
Factory Lane
Oldport
OL1 9BD

22 London Road,
Sidford,
HB3 9EL

4th June

Dear Sir or Madam,

It was my birthday last week. One of my friends at my party gave me a box of chocolates. They were made at your factory. I opened the box to try them when my friends had gone. I was very upset because the chocolates had gone all white. My mum said I mustn't eat them. Dad said the chocolates were stale but the 'best before' date is not until next August. My friend got the chocolates from Mrs Brown's sweet shop in the High Street.

Could you tell me why the chocolates went white? My dad says I should get a refund, but I would prefer another box of chocolates.

Yours faithfully,

Jason Cross

Answer these questions in sentences.

1   When did Jason get the box of chocolates?

_____

2   Why did Jason's friend give him the chocolates?

_____

3   Why do you think he opened the box after his friends had gone?

_____

4   How long will it be before the chocolates are out of date?

_____

5   What would Jason get if he got a refund?

_____

New home

Flat 8, Castle Hill,
Henford, BD8 1QE

8th September

Dear Tom

Thank you for your letter. Your new guinea pig sounds nice. It was a shame about Ginger getting out of his cage. I expect he went under your shed.

Our new flat is all right. It is at the top of the building so we have to use the stairs or the lift to get to it. I can't have a guinea pig or anything. I can only have a goldfish or a budgie. Mum says we can all have a goldfish each but you can't do much with a goldfish. My Gran says she will get me a budgie. She says I can teach it to talk.

I'm glad you can come to stay at half term. Bring your skateboard. There is a special place in the park near here for us to use – it has lots of ramps and things!

Love
Chris

Answer these questions in sentences.

1   What sort of animal do you think Ginger was?

_____

2   What are the two ways for Chris to get to his new home?

_____

3   Why can't Chris have a dog or a cat for a pet? Do you think this is fair?

_____

4   Where is a good place to skateboard near Chris? What makes it good?

_____

5   What would you like or dislike about living high up in a flat?

_____

Name _____   Date _____

Project

The Dog Warden,
Stanworth District Council,
Stanworth,
SH1 1XM

St Mark's C.E. School, Stanworth, SH10 6OJ

10th March

Dear Sir or Madam,
Our class is going to do a project next term on pets and how to look after them.
My group is going to find out about dogs. Some of the things we want to find
out about are where are the best places to buy a dog, how to keep a dog healthy
and to train it. We also want to know about the different breeds and what kind of
dog would make the best family pet.
   We would like you to come to our school to talk to us about dog ownership
and training. Please could you let us know when you could come? We
would like it to be before the end of term if you can.
      Yours faithfully,
      Emma Reed

Answer these questions in sentences.

1 What is the class project about?

_____

2 What does Emma's group want to find out?

_____

3 What other animals could be included in the project?

_____

4 Why do you think Emma wrote to a Dog Warden?

_____

5 Write a question you think the group might ask the Dog Warden.

_____

Name _____ Date _____

Diagnostic assessment – Dialogue

Never Kiss Frogs!

She looked around – there was no one there. But Gail knew she was being watched. Then she saw it. Sitting under a dock leaf, big beady eyes staring, breathing in and out, was the biggest, fattest, grottiest-looking frog. Then the frog spoke.

"Sweet lady. Please have pity on me."

"You what?" said Gail. She didn't mean to be rude. Her mother was always trying to get her to say "Pardon". But it just came out.

"Have pity on a poor creature in distress," said the frog.

Gail crouched down and very carefully put her face a few inches from the frog's. "My story," said the frog, "is a long and sad one …".

But Gail couldn't wait. She knew what she had to do. She squeezed up her mouth and gave the frog a great big kiss right in the middle of his sentence. There was a sudden noise like the sound of a blown-up paper bag bursting. Then Gail found herself staring not at the frog any more, but at a pair of highly polished leather boots.

by Robert Leeson

---

1   What made Gail look around?

_____

2   Where did Gail see the frog?

                                          Set A

_____ pages 17 - 18

3   What did the frog look like?

_____

---

4   What gave Gail such a surprise?

_____

5   Why did Gail's mother think she was rude sometimes?   **Set B**

_____ pages 19 - 20

6   What do you think might have happened to the frog?

_____

---

7   What happened after Gail kissed the frog?

_____

8   Who do you think was wearing the leather boots?   **Set C**

_____ pages 21 - 22

9   What do you think might happen next?

_____

Name _____ Date _____

Burglar Bill

One night Burglar Bill is working in a little street
behind the police station. When he comes to the first
house he climbs in through the bathroom window
and shines his torch around.

   "That's a nice toothbrush," says Burglar
Bill. "I'll have that!" And he puts it into
his sack.

   When he comes to the second house
he climbs in through the kitchen
window and shines his torch around.

   "That's a nice tin of beans!" says
Burglar Bill. "I'll have that!" And he
puts it into his sack.

   When he comes to the sixteenth
house, he stops. There on the front step
is a big brown box with little holes in it.

   "That's a nice big brown box with
little holes in it," says Burglar Bill.
"I'll have that!"

   In the distance the town hall clock strikes
five. "Time to stop work," says Burglar Bill.

by Allan and Janet Ahlberg

Complete these sentences.

1 Burglar Bill's job is _____ .

2 Burglar Bill is talking to _____ .

3 Burglar Bill does his work _____ .

4 The second thing Burglar Bill puts in his sack is

   _____ .

5 On the front step was _____ .

Name _____ Date _____

Rabbit and Tiger go fishing

Tiger: I'm glad you asked me to come fishing, Rabbit.
          We are going to have some fun!

Rabbit: I am going to catch lots of fish and take them
          home to feed my hungry children.

Tiger: (He gives Rabbit a sly look.) Big one for me,
          Rabbit, little one for you!

Rabbit: (He looks very surprised.) What did you say, Tiger?

Tiger: (He stares hard at Rabbit.) I said big for me,
          little for you. I'll have all the big fish and
          you can have all the little fish.

Rabbit: (He looks very cross.) All right,
          Tiger, here you are. (He gives
          his big fish to Tiger.) Let's
          come fishing again tomorrow.

Tiger: (He looks surprised and
          pleased.) Yes, let's! I'd like
          that!

Answer the questions in sentences.

1   How many characters are in the play?

   _____

2   What has Rabbit asked Tiger to do?

   _____

3   Why does Rabbit want to go fishing?

   _____

4   Who does Tiger say would get all the little fish?

   _____

5   Is Tiger being fair? What do you think Rabbit should do?

   _____

Name _____ Date _____

There's a Troll at the bottom of my garden

"What are you doing here?" asked Patrick.

"My rickedy, rackedy bridge was pulled down," the Troll said sadly. "And a big road was built. There were lots and lots of cars. It wasn't a nice place for a Troll any more. So I left and walked and walked. In the end I saw this shed and came in. Now I don't know what to do or where to go."

The Troll started to cry.

"Don't cry," said Patrick. "You can stay in this shed. We won't tell anybody. And we'll bring you an ice-cream every day."

"You are nice," said the Troll. "I am very grateful. This is the first nice thing that has happened to me for ages."

So the children saved their pocket money and spent it all on ice-cream for the Troll. In return he told them stories of the old days, when he had been very wicked.

"I used to sit under my rickedy, rackedy bridge," he told them, "and I would scare everyone who wanted to cross over. It was good fun."

by Ann Jungman

Answer the questions in sentences.

1 What had happened to the Troll to make him sad?

_____

2 Where did Patrick find the Troll?

_____

3 Why did Patrick and his friends help the Troll?

_____

4 What did the Troll do in return for the children being nice to him?

_____

5 Do you think the Troll has changed since the old days? How?

_____

The pet shop robbery

Scene: A policeman interviewing a pet shop owner.

Policeman:	Well, madam, I hear a robbery has taken place.
Shop Owner:	Indeed it has! A man came in at about 2 o'clock with a young boy. Whilst I was with another customer, the boy let three gerbils out of the cage.
Policeman:	What happened then?
Shop Owner:	Well, while I was chasing round trying to catch the gerbils, the man grabbed the cage with my prize parrot in it and ran off with the boy following.
Policeman:	Can you describe this man?
Shop Owner:	I certainly can! He was wearing a dark blue polo-neck sweater and a pair of jeans with patches on the knees. His hair was bright red and curly – I am sure it was a wig!
Policeman:	What about the boy?
Shop Owner:	He was wearing a red sweatshirt and blue jeans.
Policeman:	Thank you, Mrs Mole, it shouldn't be too hard to find a boy and a man with a parrot in a cage.
Shop Owner:	Well, the parrot will help! It knows the address and telephone number of the shop. It can talk, you see, and it was shouting as the man ran off with it.

Answer these questions in sentences.

1   What is the name of the shop owner?

_____

2   Why do you think the boy let the gerbils out?

_____

3   Why was the man wearing a wig?

_____

4   What is special about the parrot?

_____

5   Do you think it will be easy to find the robber and the parrot? Why?

_____

Name _____ Date _____

Training Zero to beg

"Come on, then," Jack said. "Let's start the
training. Here."

He handed up the bag of biscuits. He himself then
crouched on all fours beside Zero, who was dozing.

"Hey, Zero!"

Zero opened his eyes and his ears pricked up slightly.

"Now – watch me!"

Zero yawned hugely and moved to a sitting position. He looked dazed.

"Now," whispered Jack to Uncle Parker, "you say 'UP!' and I'll sit
up and beg. If I do it and he doesn't, you say, 'Good boy!' and pat my
head, and give me the biscuit."

Uncle Parker nodded. He delved in the bag and came up with a
chocolate digestive which he broke in half.

He held the biscuit aloft half-way between Jack and Zero.

"Up. Sit up. Beg. Good boy – boys, rather."

Jack accordingly crouched on his legs and held his hands drooping
forward in imitation of front paws.

"Good boy!" exclaimed Uncle Parker. He patted Jack on the head
and held out the biscuit. Jack opened his mouth and Uncle Parker
pushed the half digestive into it. It nearly choked him. He looked
sideways to see that Zero was looking distinctly interested.

by Helen Cresswell

Answer these questions in sentences.

1   Why does Jack crouch down next to Zero?

_____

2   What are Jack's instructions to Uncle Parker?

_____

3   What does Jack hope Zero will do?

_____

4   What do you think Zero finds most interesting about his training?

_____

5   What is meant by 'Zero was looking distinctly interested'?

_____

A surprise from the past

Scene: Two boys and a girl in a forest clearing. All have spades.
One boy has a metal detector which is signalling a find.

Ben: Hurray! At last we've found some treasure!

Sally: Let's hope it doesn't turn out to be a rusty
            old chain like the one you found last time.

Pradeep: That chain will be useful, just you see!
            Come on! Let's get digging. Careful now!
            We don't want to cause any damage to
            whatever it is.
            (The children start digging in the loose
            sandy soil.)

Sally: I'm sure my spade caught something.
            We'd better be careful!
            (The children continue to dig, but more
            cautiously.)

Ben: It's coming clear! Whatever is it? It's got a sharp point
            one end and sort of fins like a dart at the other.

Sally: Oh no! I bet it's an old bomb! It looks like one I've seen
            in a film.
            (The two boys peer anxiously at the object.)

Pradeep: I think you're right. Now what should we do?

Answer these questions in sentences.

1   What are the children doing?

_____

2   Have they had much success so far?

_____

3   Why do they need to be careful with their spades?

_____

4   Why are they worried about the object they find?

_____

5   What advice would you give to them? What should they do?

_____

Name _____ Date _____

Diagnostic assessment – Narrative

Hot Dog was looking for somewhere to rest. He found a hole.
Hot Dog explored the hole. It went deep underground.
There was a strong smell and it was a dog smell.

    Hot Dog came out backwards – very fast. After him came
a water rat. It was the same size as him – but its teeth
were bigger. Hot Dog ran off.

    By now Hot Dog was worn out. He wished he was at
home in Mrs Harris's hat. Just then a bird flew out of a tree. A big
black and white bird. It was a magpie. It spotted Hot Dog's collar.

    Magpies like bright things. The magpie carried
Hot Dog up in the air.

by Rose Impey

1 What was Hot Dog looking for? _____

2 What did he find? _____

3 How was Hot Dog feeling? _____

Set A

pages
24 - 25

4 Describe the place Hot Dog explored.

_____

5 Why didn't Hot Dog like this place?

_____

6 Why do you think Hot Dog was worn out?

Set B

pages
26 - 27

7 Why does Hot Dog wish he was home?

_____

8 The magpie is attracted to Hot Dog's collar – why?

_____

9 What do you think will happen to Hot Dog?

_____

Set C

pages
28 - 29

Name _____ Date _____

Winnie the Witch

Winnie the Witch lived in a black
house in the forest.
The house was black on the outside
and black on the inside.
The carpets were black.
The chairs were black.
The bed was black and it had black
sheets and black blankets.
Even the bath was black.

Winnie lived in her black house with
her cat, Wilbur. He was black too.
And that is how the trouble began.

by Korky Paul and Valerie Thomas

Answer these questions in sentences.

1   Whose house is in the forest?

_____

2   What is unusual about the house?

_____

3   What did Winnie the Witch call her cat?

_____

4   The cat is black – why could this be a problem?

_____

5   What kind of trouble might there be at Winnie's house?

_____

Juggling with Jeremy

Jeremy liked the supermarket.

He liked to push the trolley. He liked to bump other people's trolleys. But today he just wanted to juggle.

Mum bought fish and biscuits and beans. Then she stopped by the egg counter. She opened a box of eggs. She looked at the eggs to check they weren't cracked.

Jeremy took three eggs. They were quite a good weight. Jeremy tossed the eggs into the air.

One came down on the supermarket floor – SPLAT!

Another came down on the head of the supermarket manager – DOUBLE SPLAT!

Jeremy managed to catch the other egg.

by Chris d'lacey

Answer these questions in sentences.

1   What did Jeremy like to do with the shopping trolley?

_____

2   What did Jeremy want to do on this visit to the supermarket?

_____

3   Why did Mum look at the eggs?

_____

4   Why did Jeremy juggle with the eggs?

_____

5   How do you think the supermarket manager felt when the egg landed on his head?

_____

Name _____ Date _____

At the beach

Alice and Emil had been invited
to spend the day at their Aunt
Odile's house. Their cousins Eve,
Laurie and Biba were waiting for them so that they
could all go to the beach.

They built a huge sandcastle. It was a perfect day.

Instead of going home to tea with the others, Alice
and Emil stayed behind on the beach.

They borrowed Biba's rubber boat so they
could get close to the people who were fishing.
They didn't realise that the wind had changed
direction and that they were being blown
towards the open sea.

On the beach, nobody saw what
had happened. Anyway, it was
getting late and all the bathers were
packing up to go home.

by Philippe Dumas

Answer these questions in sentences.

1   Where did Alice and Emil meet their cousins?

_____

2   Was the beach sandy or stony?

_____

3   What did the five children do together?

_____

4   Why was it a problem when the wind changed direction?

_____

5   What do you think happened to Alice and Emil?

_____

Tilly's house

Upstairs in the doll's house there lived a family of wooden dolls. Father worked in his study all day, while Mother did the mending in the parlour. The two children played in the nursery on the floor above. Downstairs in the kitchen, Cook prepared the meals, and gave orders to Tilly, the kitchen maid.

Poor Tilly! Every day she got up at five to clean out the grates and lay the fires. She cleared the breakfast table, made the beds, and swept and cleaned and scrubbed and polished all day long. After supper she did the washing up and mopped the kitchen floor. And all the time Cook nagged at her, and shouted at her, and told her she must work still harder.

"I wouldn't mind how hard I worked if I had a home of my own," Tilly said to herself one night as she washed a pile of dirty dishes. "But I'm sick and tired of Cook ordering me around all day, with never a word of thanks."

Just then Cook cried out, "Tilly! Make sure you do the ironing before you go to bed!"

by Faith Jacques

Answer these questions in sentences.

1   How many dolls lived in the doll's house?

_____

2   Did Tilly like working in the house? Why?

_____

3   Write down four of the jobs Tilly did each day.

_____

4   Write down the words you think would best describe Cook.

_____

5   Why do you think Cook shouted at Tilly?

_____

The Iron Man

In his pocket, among other things, he had a long nail
and a knife. He took these out. Did he dare? His idea
frightened him. In the silent dusk, he tapped the nail
and the knife blade together.
Clink, clink, clink!
   At the sound of the metal, the Iron Man's hands
became still. After a few seconds, he slowly turned his
head and the headlamp eyes shone towards Hogarth.
   Again, Clink, clink, clink! went the nail on the knife.
   Slowly, the Iron Man took three strides towards
Hogarth, and again stopped. It was now quite dark.
The headlamps shone red. Hogarth pressed close to the
tree trunk. Between him and the Iron Man lay the wide lid of the trap.
   Clink, clink, clink! Again he tapped the nail on the knife.
   And now the Iron Man was coming. Hogarth could feel the earth
shaking under the weight of his footsteps. Was it too late to run?
Hogarth stared at the Iron Man, looming, searching towards him for
the taste of the metal that had made that inviting sound.
   Clink, clink, clink! went the nail on the knife. And CRASSSHHH!
   The Iron Man vanished. He was in the pit. The Iron Man had fallen
into the pit. Hogarth went close. The earth was shaking as the Iron
Man struggled underground.

by Ted Hughes

Answer these questions in sentences.

1   What time of the day was it?

_____

2   Why did Hogarth tap the nail and knife blade together?

_____

3   Describe what you think the Iron Man looked like.

_____

4   Why did Hogarth press himself close to the tree?

_____

5   How do you think Hogarth felt when the Iron Man vanished?

_____

The BFG

When she reached the curtains, Sophie hesitated. She longed to duck underneath them and lean out of the window to see what the world looked like now that the witching hour was at hand.

She listened again. Everywhere it was deathly still.

The longing to look out became so strong she couldn't resist it. Quickly, she ducked under the curtains and leaned out of the window.

In the silvery moonlight, the village street she knew so well seemed completely different. The houses looked bent and crooked, like houses in a fairy tale. Everything was pale and ghostly and milky-white.

Across the road, she could see Mrs Rance's shop, where you bought buttons and wool and bits of elastic. It didn't look real. There was something dim and misty about that too.

Sophie allowed her eye to travel further and further down the street.

Suddenly she froze. There was something coming up the street on the opposite side.

It was something black ...

Something tall and black ...

Something very tall and very black and very thin.

by Roald Dahl

Answer these questions in sentences.

1   What time of the day do you think 'the witching hour' is?

_____

2   What made the village street look different? In what way?

_____

3   What did Sophie see that startled her?

_____

4   What do you think was coming up the street?

_____

5   How would you have felt if you had been Sophie?

_____

Name _____ Date _____

Diagnostic assessment – Biography

Mr Hoover and the vacuum cleaner

In 1901, Mr Booth invented a very big vacuum cleaner that went along the street and a long pipe was put through the windows in a house. It was a very noisy machine and frightened the horses.

In America, Mr Spangler invented a small vacuum cleaner. It had a brush to help get the dirt out and it had a dust bag. Mr Spangler was very poor and he showed his invention to Mr Hoover. Mr Hoover bought the idea of the small vacuum cleaner from Mr Spangler in 1907.

Mr Hoover started to make vacuum cleaners. People were able to have one of their own. Very soon vacuum cleaners were known as 'hoovers' and the word 'hoovering' was invented.

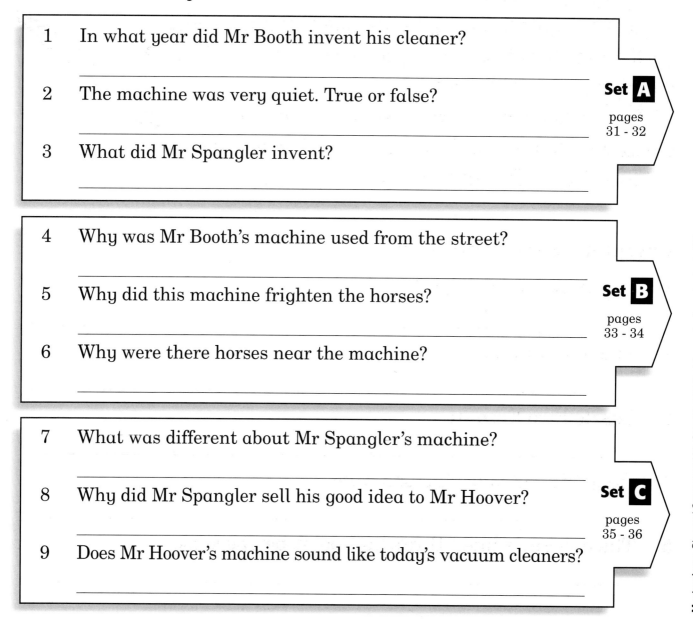

1   In what year did Mr Booth invent his cleaner?

   _____

2   The machine was very quiet. True or false?   **Set A**
                                                               pages
   _____   31 - 32

3   What did Mr Spangler invent?

   _____

4   Why was Mr Booth's machine used from the street?

   _____

5   Why did this machine frighten the horses?   **Set B**
                                                               pages
   _____   33 - 34

6   Why were there horses near the machine?

   _____

7   What was different about Mr Spangler's machine?

   _____

8   Why did Mr Spangler sell his good idea to Mr Hoover?   **Set C**
                                                               pages
   _____   35 - 36

9   Does Mr Hoover's machine sound like today's vacuum cleaners?

   _____

Name _____ Date _____

Laszlo Biro

Before the fountain pen was invented in 1884, people used to write with a quill pen made from a goose feather. Then, in 1938, Laszlo Biro invented the ball-point pen.

Laszlo Biro lived in Budapest. He was an artist and a journalist. One day, he was watching magazines being printed. He saw that the printers used an ink that dried very quickly. This gave him an idea to invent a quick-drying ink pen.

Laszlo's brother, Georg, helped him to finish the idea for the pen. They had it made in a factory in Argentina during the Second World War.

Biro's ball-point pen was used by the RAF. The air-crews used it when they were flying. The pen did not leak like the fountain pens did.

Complete these sentences.

1 A quill pen was made from

_____ .

2 The fountain pen was invented in

_____ .

3 Laszlo Biro lived in

_____ .

4 He got the idea for his pen from

_____ .

5 The air-crews liked Biro's ball-point pen because

_____ .

Red Rum

Red Rum was a famous race horse.
He was very fast at jumping over hedges
in races called steeplechases. The best
known steeplechase is the Grand
National at Aintree, near Liverpool.

Red Rum won the Grand National
three times and came second twice.
No other horse has ever done this, so he
holds the record. When he was a foal, no one
expected him to do so well. He had a foot disease which
could have stopped him racing. Luckily his feet got better.

Red Rum was thirty years old when he died in 1995.
Everyone in the racing world was very sad. His jockeys
had been proud to ride him because he showed so much
courage. Philip Blacker, who was a jockey, made a
life-size statue of him which stands by the parade ring
at Aintree racecourse. Red Rum will never be forgotten.

Answer these questions in sentences.

1   What kind of race was Red Rum good at?

_____

2   What record did Red Rum hold?

_____

3   What could have stopped Red Rum becoming a race horse?

_____

4   Why was the racing world very sad in 1995?

_____

5   Why will Red Rum never be forgotten?

_____

Name _____ Date _____

Grock

Grock was a very famous clown in the circus.
His real name was Adrian Wettach and he
was born in Switzerland in 1880.

He joined the circus when he was twelve
years old. He worked in many different
circuses all over the world. He wore funny
clothes that were too big for him and he
wore enormous boots.

He fell over his own feet and could do
nothing right, which made people laugh.

After some years, he gave up working
in the circus and did his act on the stage
instead. He was a very good musician and
could play eight musical instruments.

Grock was interested in helping children.
When he wasn't working on the stage, he
used to give them lessons on road safety.
He was 74 years old when he decided
to retire.

Answer these questions in sentences.

1   Why do you think Adrian Wettach changed his name?

   _____

2   What do you think would be the funniest thing about Grock? Why?

   _____

3   What made Grock good at working on the stage?

   _____

4   What year did Grock stop working?

   _____

5   List four things that Grock might have taught children.

   _____

Alison Streeter

Alison Streeter was born in 1964. She started swimming because she had asthma and hoped that swimming would help her control her breathing.

She became a very good and strong swimmer and wanted to be a long-distance swimmer. Her first record-breaking swims were across the Solent to the Isle of Wight.

In 1982, she swam across the English Channel. Since then, she has been a leader in the cold and lonely sport of long-distance swimming. In 1983, she swam the Channel to France and back without stopping. This was the first time a woman had done this. Her time was faster than any other Briton. She swam the Channel four more times one way and then she swam the North Channel of the Irish Sea. In 1991, she did a three-way non-stop swim of the English Channel. It took her 34 hours 40 minutes. She was the first woman to do this. She was given the MBE for her success.

Answer these questions in sentences.

1 Why did Alison decide to start swimming?

_____

2 How old was she when she made her first Channel crossing?

_____

3 What were the two important things about Alison's swimming in 1983?

_____

4 Why do you think long-distance swimming is a 'cold and lonely sport'?

_____

5 'She was given the MBE for her success.' Explain what this means.

_____

Diana, Princess of Wales

The Honourable Diana Frances Spencer was born on 1 July, 1961 at Park House, Sandringham in Norfolk. She was the third daughter of the eighth Earl Spencer. She had two sisters, Sarah and Jane, and a younger brother, Charles.

When Diana's grandfather died, she became Lady Diana and the family moved to the ancestral home at Althorpe Hull in Northamptonshire. She first met Prince Charles in 1977 when he visited Althorpe Hall for a party. Later, when Lady Diana was older, a romance began. They were married in St Paul's Cathedral on 29th July 1981. Their first son, Prince William, was born in June 1982 and their second son, Prince Harry, was born in September 1984.

Sadly, because they were so different from each other, Princess Diana and Prince Charles grew apart. They were divorced in 1996. After the divorce, Princess Diana put her energies into her work for charities. She worked with the Red Cross to ban land mines. Photographs of her shaking hands with victims of leprosy and AIDS were shown to the world. She had a great love for children and visited those who were sick. She also visited people ill with cancer and helped the homeless through the charity Centrepoint.

Princess Diana died after a tragic car accident in 1997. She will always be remembered for her exceptional care for others.

Answer the questions in sentences.

1   How many brothers and sisters did Diana have?

_____

2   How many Earls Spencer had there been before her father?

_____

3   How much older than Prince Harry is Prince William?

_____

4   Why do you think she wanted to ban land mines?

_____

5   How do you think Princess Diana will be remembered by most people?

_____

Charles Darwin

Natural history was Charles Darwin's greatest interest. When he was 22, he joined a group of scientists for an expedition on a ship called HMS Beagle. The ship set sail for South America in December 1831. They reached Brazil in the spring of 1832.

They sailed south down the coast, exploring as they went. Darwin wrote notes about everything he saw. He was amazed at the number of different birds and flowers with their dazzling colours. He made a huge collection of rocks, fossils, plants, birds, animals and shells.

In September 1835, they reached the Galapagos Islands. These islands are 600 miles off the north-west coast of South America. Here Darwin saw plants and animals that are not found anywhere else.

HMS Beagle got back to England in October 1836. In 1859, Darwin published his famous book, 'The Origin of Species'. This explained how he thought life on Earth had evolved over millions of years.

Answer the questions in sentences.

1   Why is Charles Darwin famous?

_____

2   Why did he join the expedition in 1831?

_____

3   What do you think were Darwin's main aims on his trip?

_____

4   Give at least two reasons why the Galapagos Islands are very unusual.

_____

5   Why do you think it took Darwin so long to write his book?

_____

Name _____ Date _____

Diagnostic assessment – Instructions

The sentences in each set are mixed up. Read them carefully and write the letters in the correct order.

Feeding the cat
A Take the lid off the tin.
B Call your cat.
C Put the cat food in the dish.
D Get a tin of cat food and a dish.

Set A
pages
38 - 39

_____ _____ _____ _____

Shopping
A If they haven't one, a white one will do.
B Would you go to the shop for me please?
C Martin, we have used up all the bread.
D Take my purse and the basket with you.
E Get us a brown loaf.

Set B
pages
40 - 41

_____ _____ _____ _____ _____

Directions
A The tennis court is behind the village hall, next to the football pitch.
B Turn left just after the school.
C Collect the tennis court key from the house by the village hall.
D Carry on down this road until you come to the school on your right.
E Go about 400 metres along the road until you come to the village hall which will be on your left.

Set C
pages
42 - 43

_____ _____ _____ _____ _____

Draw a map to show the way to the tennis court.

Name _____   Date _____

Uno's visit

Read the story and then complete the picture.

Uno landed his rocket on the top of the hill next to an old barn.
He got out. There were six woolly sheep eating grass in front of
the barn.

Uno looked down the hill and saw four brown cows in the field by
the river. Behind the cows was a big tree. The tree had a big bird's nest
in it. Three ducks were swimming down the river.

A red tractor and trailer was going over the bridge. A sheep dog
was riding on the trailer. Two boys were sitting on the river bank
across from the cows. The boys were fishing and they each had a
fishing rod.

Uno wondered what the boys were doing. "I'll go down and ask
them," he said.

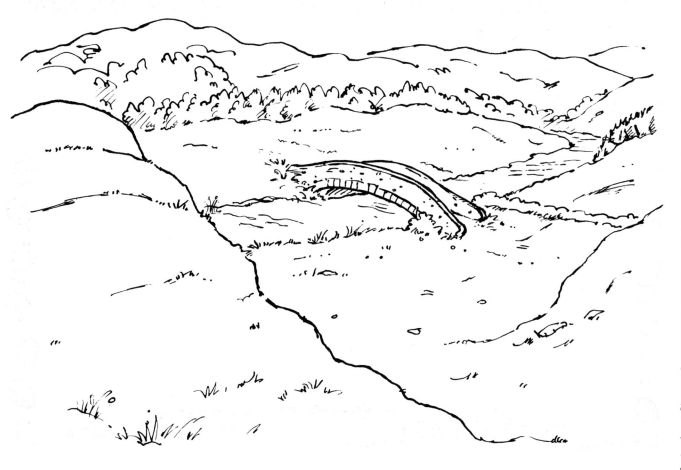

A *Masterpieces:* **Comprehension** INSTRUCTIONS   LOWER JUNIOR

How to make a cress man

1 These instructions are in the wrong order. Number the steps in the right order to make the cress man. The first one has been numbered for you.

☐ Keep the tissue damp and wait for the 'hair' to grow.

☐ Draw a face and ears on the egg shell with coloured felt-tipped-pens.

☐ Stand the filled egg shell in an egg cup and put it on the window sill.

1 Carefully cut the top off a boiled egg and eat the egg. Clean out the egg shell well.

☐ Fill the egg shell three quarters full with a crumpled damp tissue or damp cotton wool.

☐ Sprinkle cress seeds over the surface of the damp tissue or cotton wool.

2 Draw and colour a picture of the finished cress man.

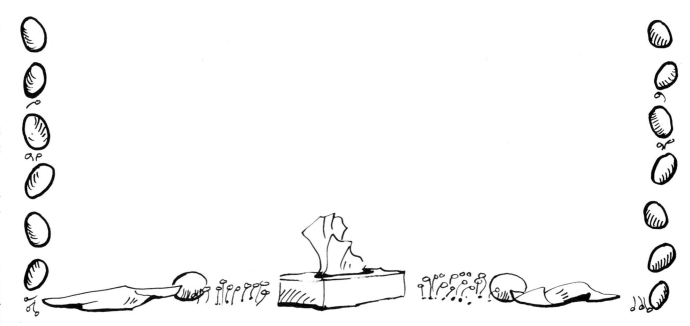

Raisin clusters

These instructions are in the wrong order. Read the sentences carefully, then write the letters in the right order at the bottom of the page.

A Heat the water on a hotplate or on the stove until the chocolate melts. Do not stir.

B Pour cold water into a saucepan. Put the saucepan on the stove.

C Add more cornflakes and stir again. Keep adding cornflakes until you have a nice chocolate-covered mixture.

D Choose a basin that will fit over the saucepan and is big enough to mix everything together in.

E Put teaspoonfuls of the mixture on a baking tray or plate. Use the teaspoon to pat into 'cluster' shapes. Leave until the clusters are hard and then put them on a serving plate.

F SAFETY NOTE: raisin clusters should be made with adult supervision!

G Break about 50g of chocolate into the basin. Stand the basin over the saucepan and make sure it is steady.

H Turn off the heat and lift the basin from the saucepan. Use oven gloves or a thick cloth. Add about 50g of raisins and some of the cornflakes to the chocolate. Stir with a wooden spoon.

_____ _____ _____ _____ _____ _____ _____ _____

Name _____ Date _____

Visit to Rudford

1   Read the letter, then on the map below trace the way Rosie will
    have to go.

6 Whitefield Road
Rudford
RF2 6XS
6th February

Dear Rosie,
   I am very pleased you can come to stay next week. I will have to look after my new puppy so I can't meet you from the bus station. Never mind, here are some directions to my house.
   When you come out of the bus station, turn right and walk up Westbury Road. Take the first right turn into Albert Street and then the second left turn into Edward Street. Go down Edward Street, cross over Bishops Road and go on until you come to Queens Road. Turn right into Queens Road and then left into Whitefield Road. My house is number 6 on the right-hand side. I will put a yellow balloon on the gate post so you will see where the house is. Don't forget your swimming things!
            Love,
               Amy

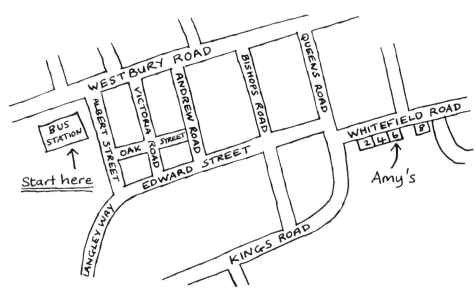

2   Now, on the back of this sheet, write out the instructions for a
    different way to Amy's house from the bus station.

Name _____ Date _____

Modelling with papier-mâché

These instructions are in the wrong order. Read the sentences carefully, then write the letters in the right order at the bottom of the page.

A   Add water (a little at a time) and go on squeezing until the paper is mushy and feels sticky. If it does not feel sticky, add more paste.

B   Put the pieces into another bowl and sprinkle a cupful of wallpaper paste over them.

C   The paper can now be moulded into any shape; heads for puppets or dolls, flat trays or bowls. Make sure the base is flat if making a bowl so that it does not wobble!

D   Put the pieces into a bowl and pour water over them. Make them very wet and then squeeze them as dry as possible.

E   Collect together an old newspaper, 2 large bowls, a cupful of wallpaper paste and a jug of water.

F   Mix the paper and paste with your hands and make sure each piece of paper is covered with paste.

G   Put the shape in a warm dry place to dry slowly. After a week, it should be dry and you can paint and varnish it.

H   Tear the newspaper into small pieces.

____ ____ ____ ____ ____ ____ ____ ____

The toy cupboard

1   Read through the story and then draw pictures on the shelves to show
    what the cupboard looked like after Hugo had tidied it.

2   Label the boxes and jars.

Hugo looked in his toy cupboard. What a mess! He decided to tidy it.
The cupboard had three shelves and doors that opened wide.

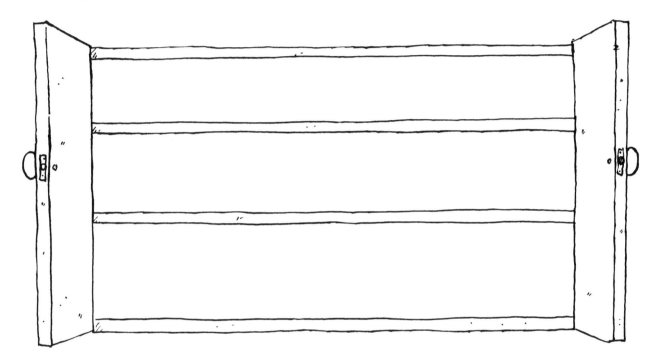

Hugo took everything out of the cupboard. Then, on the left-hand side of
the top shelf he put his two torches. These were separated from a box of bits
and pieces by a tin of felt-tipped pens. Next came his boat, standing to the
left of a jar of marbles. In the right-hand corner he put his jar of shells.
    The middle shelf was all boxes apart from a microscope which stood in
the middle. To the left of the microscope he put three games – draughts,
ludo and snakes and ladders. Between the games and the microscope he put
his box of farm animals. On the other side of the microscope he put his box
of zoo animals. His four jigsaw puzzles filled the rest of the shelf.
    At the right-hand side of the bottom shelf he put two big books. To the
left of the books, he put a box full of little cars. Next came his fire engine.
He squeezed his tractor in between a tub of Lego and his fire engine. He put
two videos on top of the games on the middle shelf.

Name _____ Date _____

Diagnostic assessment – Information

Helicopters were invented in the 1930s. They are very useful aircraft. The wings of most aircraft are fixed on each side of the aircraft and do not move. Instead of fixed wings, a helicopter has rotor blades fixed on top. These rotate and act like spinning wings.

Unlike aeroplanes, helicopters can hover above the ground, so they are very useful in rescue work. The pilot can hover over a disaster or accident. Trapped and injured people can be lifted off cliff faces or mountains using a long cable. People can be snatched out of the sea if they are in difficulties and rescued from the tops of burning buildings.

Because they can fly close to the ground, helicopters are often used to search for people who are lost in the countryside. The police use helicopters to search for criminals because they have a 'bird's eye view'.

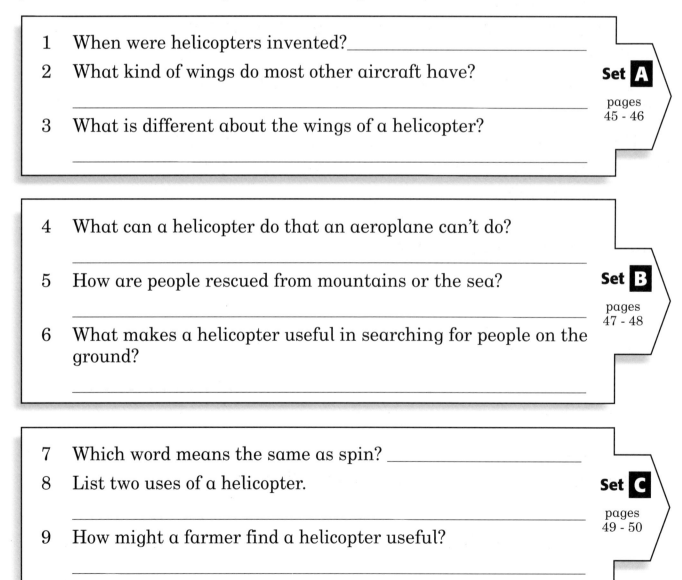

1   When were helicopters invented?_____

2   What kind of wings do most other aircraft have?

_____

Set A

pages
45 - 46

3   What is different about the wings of a helicopter?

_____

4   What can a helicopter do that an aeroplane can't do?

_____

5   How are people rescued from mountains or the sea?

_____

Set B

pages
47 - 48

6   What makes a helicopter useful in searching for people on the ground?

_____

7   Which word means the same as spin? _____

8   List two uses of a helicopter.

_____

Set C

pages
49 - 50

9   How might a farmer find a helicopter useful?

_____

Hot air balloons

One day, over two hundred years ago, two French brothers were sitting in front of the fire. One of the brothers, Joseph, noticed that if paper was put on the fire, the burned paper was sent flying up from the flames. They had made an important discovery: hot air rises.

To make sure they were right, Joseph and his brother Etienne trapped hot air in a bag. When they let go of the bag, it floated upwards.

The Montgolfier brothers went on to make the first hot air balloon. Their balloon was an open-ended bag. A fire burned under the open end of the bag to keep it filled with hot air.

The first hot air balloon to carry people was launched in 1783. The problem with balloons was that they could go only where the wind blew them.

Complete these sentences.

1 The two brothers were called

_____ .

2 When Joseph burned paper on the fire it

_____ .

3 The important discovery was

_____ .

4 The air was kept hot in the first balloon by

_____ .

5 The problem with going somewhere in a hot air balloon was

_____ .

Toads

When you first see a toad it looks a bit like a frog. If you look carefully, you will soon see the differences. A toad does not leap and jump like a frog. It crawls along or makes very short jumps on all four feet.

Its skin is brown like the colour of soil. It is covered in bumps like pimples. Its brown, lumpy skin makes the toad hard to see on the ground. It can stay very, very still for a long time. This helps it to look like a lump of earth.

Toads eat flies, worms, caterpillars, snails and even small mice. In the spring, female toads walk back to the ponds where they were born to lay their eggs in long strings called toadspawn. The eggs hatch into tadpoles which change into baby toads after eleven or twelve weeks.

Answer these questions in sentences.

1   What other creature does a toad look like?

_____

2   How does a frog move over the ground?

_____

3   Why might a toad be difficult to see?

_____

4   How do you think the toad tricks animals that might eat it?

_____

5   How are toads' eggs different from chickens' eggs?

_____

Name _____ Date _____

Heraldry

Hundreds of years ago, knights wore armour to protect themselves from being hurt in battle. The trouble was they all looked alike and it was difficult for a knight to see who his friends were. To avoid being mistaken for the enemy, they painted patterns and designs on their shields and the flags of their lances.

Each knight chose his own design, which was plain and simple so that they were easy to see and recognise and different from others.

Only a small number of bright colours were used for the designs because they were easier to see at a distance. The colours were red, blue, black, green and purple, on a background of yellow or white.

Men called heralds made a record of each design so that it would not be forgotten. They also made sure that no two knights had the same design. The designs became known as heraldry.

Write true or false by each statement below.

1   Before heraldry, the knights in armour all looked alike.   _____

2   Patterns were painted all over their armour.   _____

3   The heralds helped the knights to put on their armour.   _____

4   Bright colours were used in the designs because the knights liked them.   _____

5   A knight kept to the same design so everyone would know him.   _____

Otters

The otter belongs to the same family as the badger, but the otter lives by a river. Their home is called a 'holt'. They like to eat fish, frogs and other water animals.

When the sun has set, the otter wakes up and begins to hunt for food. To catch its food it has to be able to swim well. It has short, strong legs with webbed feet and its tail is long and thick. These help it to be a very good swimmer. The otter's fur is so thick that its skin does not get wet when it swims.

When the otter dives, it keeps its eyes open so that it can find and catch a fish. It brings the fish ashore to eat.

In the spring, the female otter has two or three babies called 'cubs'. She keeps them in a nest or 'holt' made from rushes and grass. The nest is lined with the soft purple flowers from reeds. Both parents find food for the babies until they are old enough to fend for themselves.

Answer these questions in sentences.

1   What is the name for an otter's home?

_____

2   How does the otter get its food?

_____

3   Why might the otter be a better swimmer than you?

_____

4   Where does the otter eat its food?

_____

5   Do you think the otter's nest is comfortable? Why?

_____

Name _____ Date _____

Kellogg's Corn flakes

Over one hundred years ago, in 1894, the
Kellogg brothers – Will Keith Kellogg and
Dr John Harvey Kellogg – were in charge of
a 'sanatorium' in Battle Creek, Michigan,
USA. It was a hospital health resort where
people could stay to improve their health.

   The brothers were always experimenting
with new ways to make cereals tasty and easy to digest. One of their
first experiments was with wheat. They boiled the wheat and passed
it through rollers. One day, a batch of the dough they had made was
left out overnight accidentally. When the dough was put through the
rollers the next day, it came off the rollers in large, thin flakes.

   The brothers decided to see what would happen if the flakes
were baked. They were surprisingly tasty. The flakes were very
popular with the people staying in the 'sanatorium', who, when they
went home, asked for supplies of them to be sent by post. So, the
first Kellogg's flakes were sold by mail order.

   Four years later, Will Keith Kellogg tried using corn instead of
wheat to make the flakes. He found that the corn flakes tasted even
better. In 1906, he started his own factory. To stop people copying
his idea, he had his signature printed on each packet of the corn
flakes produced in his factory. Twenty years later, Kellogg's corn
flakes were first exported to Britain.

Write true or false by each of these sentences.

1   Corn flakes were invented accidentally.   _____

2   The flakes were first sold in a shop at the sanatorium.   _____

3   People stayed at the sanatorium to learn about making cereals. _____

4   People in Britain bought the cornflakes after people in the USA. _____

5   Will Keith Kellogg had his name put on the packet because he   _____
    was vain.

Name _____ Date _____

Bats

There are twelve different types of bats that live in Britain. While most bats are not often seen, the Long-Eared Bat can be seen almost anywhere.

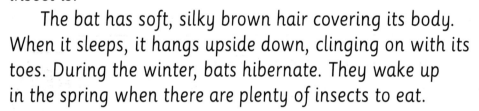

Birds and bats are the only creatures that have backbones and can fly. Unlike birds, however, bats can no longer move about on the ground, because all four of their limbs have been adapted for flying. All bats are nocturnal. They like to eat insects. They find their food by sending out ultrasonic squeaks that echo, bouncing off the insects and back to the bat's ears, which are huge. This tells the bat where the insect is.

The bat has soft, silky brown hair covering its body. When it sleeps, it hangs upside down, clinging on with its toes. During the winter, bats hibernate. They wake up in the spring when there are plenty of insects to eat.

Answer these questions in sentences.

1   Does the Long-Eared Bat live only in certain parts of the country?

_____

2   Why can't bats walk or hop on the ground like birds?

_____

3   What does 'nocturnal' mean?

_____

4   Could bats live among trees? In what way?

_____

5   Use your own words to describe how bats find food.

_____

_____

Name _____ Date _____

Diagnostic assessment – Notices, lists and news

Radio Times – *Wednesday*

Channel 4

9.45am Book Box (ages 7–9) Thief!
(Part 1)

10.00 Stage Two Science
(ages 7–11)
Life Processes: Family groups

10.15 TV: Friend or Foe? (ages 9–13)
Taste and Violence

10.45 GNVQ: Is it for You?
(ages 16–19)
Leisure and Tourism

11.07 Lost Animals (all ages)
Arizona Jaguar – A look at
extinct animals

11.15 The Mix (ages 7–10)
Songs and Sounds by Leaps
and Bounds

11.30 Rat-a-Tat-Tat (ages 4–6)
"Only Joking!" laughed the
Lobster

11.45 Backtracks (ages 9–14)
Science Fiction

1 Would a child of five years watch Rat-a-Tat-Tat? _____

2 Which programme could children of any age enjoy?

_____

3 What time is a music programme broadcast? _____

Set A

pages
52 - 53

4 Are the programmes arranged by age? _____

5 Are there fiction and non-fiction programmes? _____

6 Which extinct animal could you learn about? _____

Set B

pages
54 - 55

7 What kind of programme do you think Book Box is?

_____

8 If you weren't interested in the programme at 10am would
you like the one at 11.45? Why?

_____

9 Does Channel 4 advise on careers? _____

Set C

pages
56 - 57

Name _____ Date _____

The pet show

A Grand Pet Show

will be held at
Newton Primary School
on
Saturday afternoon

All Pets are Welcome!

Entrance 50p for each pet

The Show opens at 2 o'clock
The pets will be judged
by
Mr Cyril Bird

Teas, Ices and Soft Drinks will be on sale.

1   Complete this invitation.

Dear Parent
The children and staff at _____ school invite you to
their Grand _____ _____ on _____ afternoon for the
opening at _____ .
    It will cost _____ for each pet to enter. The judge will be
Mr _____ _____ .
    Teas, _____ and soft _____ will be on sale.
    Please come and join in the fun!
Yours sincerely,
Mrs Rabbitts, Headteacher

Answer these questions in sentences.

2   What kind of animals do you think would be in the show?

_____

3   Why would people take their pets?

_____

Business telephone numbers

📖 Pet shops

Bright Eyes Pets, 8 Station Road .... Oxwell 349521
Feather and Fin, 22 Burton Road .... Shipstow 228596
Harry's Pet Foods, 121 High Street .... Farley 459592
Pisces Aquatic Centre, 1 Queen Street .... Ragford 234422
Reptiles Plus, 12 Church Street .... Oxwell 347846

📖 Toy and Games shops

Acorn Model Shop, 19 High Street .... Farley 459330
Hill's Toys, 88 King Street .... Astock 860374
Ocean Kites, 66 Marine Parade............................ Buxley 203302
Software Box, 116 Friary Centre .... Rabton 860454
Party Spot, 6 The Passage................................. Rabton 860725

📖 Cycle shops

Bicycle Repairs and Hire, 21 New Street .... Farley 459206
Bikes and Trikes, 81 Albert Road .... Shipstow 228822
Forest Cycles Accessories, 61 The Square........... Astock 860119
Freewheelers Cycles, 121 London Road .... Ragford 203908
New-to-You Cycle Shop, 8 Park Road .... Buxley 203054

Write true or false by each statement below.

1   You can buy budgie food at 121 High Street, Farley.   _____

2   You can buy a goldfish in Astock.   _____

3   You can buy a new video game at Farley.   _____

4   203908 and 459330 are the numbers to ring for pet food. _____

5   You could buy a second-hand bicycle in Buxley.   _____

Heat is on cruel dog owners

HEAT IS ON CRUEL DOG OWNERS

PET OWNERS in Dorset are being warned they face six months in jail by leaving animals to suffer in cars or caravans during the hot weather.

The warning comes from the district council as it backs an RSPCA campaign to prevent dogs and other pets from baking to death.

A call has already been made to the environmental health department this year, after a dog was spotted suffering in a car.

Mark Williams, head of environmental health, said leaving windows open or putting a bowl of water in the car was not sufficient. He said those putting animals at risk face six months in jail or a fine of up to £5,000.

He added: "On a warm day, do not leave your dog in a car. If you see a distressed animal left in a parked car, please report it immediately to the police or RSPCA."

Answer these questions in sentences.

1 Why would animals suffer in hot weather?

_____

2 The RSPCA is worried only about dogs – true or false?

_____

3 Why do you think open windows and water are not enough?

_____

4 What is the biggest punishment for such owners? Do you think this is enough?

_____

5 What would you do if you saw such an animal in a hot car?

_____

Name _____ Date _____

The telephone directory

East End Newsagent
    3 Castle Street, West Foyle ....(01248) 683841

East, Dr B – Surgery,
    44 St Edwards Close, Kingsbury ....(01248) 392806

Eastbury Hotel,
    West Avenue, Shipston ....(01821) 438932

Eastern Eye Indian Takeaway
    306 High Street, Frampton ....(01248) 263646

Eatfresh Greengrocers
    12 Prince Street, Shipston ....(01821) 438923

Eaton, D. Driving Instructor
    Kingsclere,West Foyle ....(01248) 493464

Ebblake Tyres
    Unit 9, Western Ind. Estate, West Foyle ....(01248) 660622

Ebury Garden Services
    Pear Tree Cottage, North Street, Shipston ......(01821) 482569

Answer these questions in sentences.

1   Where is the Eastern Eye Indian Takeaway?

_____

2   If you were expecting visitors for lunch and needed a delivery, which number would you ring?

_____

3   Why might callers trying to telephone Eastbury Hotel get through to Eatfresh Greengrocers instead?

_____

4   What do you think 'Ind.' means?

_____

5   How many places provide food? List them.

_____

Name _____ Date _____

Holiday advertisements

Holidays

TORCROSS South Devon. Wooden bungalow. Own garden, sleeps 3/5, pets welcome, vacancies May, June, September. For details, Mrs Smith (01324) 489632

BEER Devon. Caravans, lovely views, well equipped, short walk to sea, fishing trips arranged. Vacancies July, August. Telephone (01342) 860437

HAVEN Holiday park, Chiswell Bay, South Devon. 7-berth caravan with sea views, excellent facilities. Further details telephone (01416) 732486

WOOLACOMBE North Devon. 2-bedroom self contained flat. Available June, July and September. For further details apply to Mrs Green (01462) 604181

BEACH VIEW Hotel Malston. Early September special offer. Holding Low Season Prices. 3 nights B&B – £15 per night per person. Telephone (01591) 333687

ISLE OF WIGHT Farm caravan, sleeps 6, 10 min walk to beach. Good river fishing. Vacancies August, September. Enquiries Mrs Brown. Telephone (01647) 384906

Answer these questions in sentences.

1   If you didn't want to cook for yourself where would you stay?

_____

2   If there were seven of you, why wouldn't you ring 01462 604181?

_____

3   What does the Torcross holiday offer that none of the others do?

_____

4   Where could you have a holiday caravan in July?

_____

5   What type of holiday is available in August?

_____

C *Masterpieces:* **Comprehension** NOTICES, LISTS AND NEWS   LOWER JUNIOR

Name _____ Date _____

The weather forecast

LONDON, SE ENGLAND, CEN S ENGLAND: Early mist and patches of low cloud should soon disperse to leave a warm and sunny day, but it will be cooler on the coasts. A moderate easterly wind. Max 23°C (73°F).

SW ENGLAND, CHAN ISLES, S WALES: Fine, sunny and warm. A moderate east to south-easterly wind. Cooler on east-facing coasts. Max 23°C (73°F).

MIDLANDS, E ENGLAND, E ANGLIA, NE ENGLAND, CEN N ENGLAND: Mist and low cloud will soon clear to leave sunshine. Light and variable winds. Cool on coasts with afternoon sea-breezes. Max 21°C (70°F).

N WALES, NW ENGLAND, IOM, LAKE DIST: Warm and sunny with a few harmless patches of cloud. Max temp 19–22°C. (66–72°F). Cool on coasts with afternoon sea-breezes. Max 21°C (70°F).

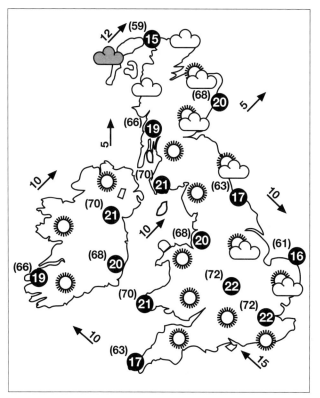

Answer these questions in sentences.

1   Which parts of Britain will be cloudy at the beginning of the day?

_____

2   In which parts of the country will it stay cloudy and wet all day?

_____

3   Which parts of the country will have the best weather?

_____

4   Will all seaside areas be good to visit with a picnic? Why?

_____

5   What will the lowest temperature be in England?

_____

Diagnostic assessment – Dialogue

Ace Dragon Ltd

by Russell Hoban

John was walking down the street when he heard something go KLONK. John looked round and saw a round iron plate in the pavement. It was like a manhole cover. On it he read: ACE DRAGON LTD.

John stamped three times on the iron cover. A voice said, "Who is it?"
John said, "John."
The voice said, "What do you want?"
John said, "I want to know what LTD means."
The voice said, "It means limited."
John said, "What does limited mean?"
The voice said, "It means I can't do everything. I can only do some things."

1 Who was walking down the street?

2 What did he hear?

3 What caused the noise?

Set A
pages 59 - 60

4 What did John see written on the iron cover?

5 Why did he stamp on the iron cover?

6 What was John told 'limited' meant?

Set B
pages 61 - 62

7 What do you think 'limited' means in this extract?

8 What or who do you think was talking to John? Give your reason for thinking this.

Set C
pages 63 - 64

9 Is this extract fiction or non-fiction? Explain your answer.

Leprechauns

According to legend, leprechauns live in Ireland. They are dressed in green, the colour of emeralds. 'Leprechaun' means very small body. They look like ugly humans. They are very good at making shoes and they are the shoemakers for the elves and fairies.

Leprechauns live on their own. They like to live in old, ruined castles. They are very quick and can vanish in the twinkling of an eye. If they know a human is near, they always disappear.

Humans try hard to catch leprechauns by creeping up behind them. Every leprechaun has a pot of gold and if one is caught, he must lead the way to where he has hidden the gold. Very few leprechauns get caught because they can trick their captor into looking the other way or letting go. As soon as that happens, they vanish into thin air.

Underline the statement that is true.

1a) Leprechauns are English.

1b) Leprechauns are Irish.

2a) Leprechauns are tall and good looking.

2b) Leprechauns are small and ugly.

3a) A leprechaun likes to live alone in a ruined castle.

3b) Leprechauns like to live together in old barns.

4a) If leprechauns see a human, they are very friendly.

4b) If leprechauns see a human, they disappear.

5a) Humans try to catch leprechauns to get their gold.

5b) Humans try to catch leprechauns to get some shoes.

Name _____   Date _____

Bathing a dog

Here is a list of things to do to bath a dog.

A   Put him in the water.
B   Dry him with the big towel and let him go.
C   Fill a bath with water and get a big towel.
D   Wash the soap off your dog.
E   Now catch the dog.
F   Rub the soap all over your dog.

1   Match the sentences to the pictures below. Write the letter for
     each sentence in the correct box.

2   On the back of this sheet, write out the steps for cleaning your
     teeth.

The silver fish

While fishing in the blue lagoon
I caught a lovely silver _____
And he spoke to _____ , "My boy," quoth he,
"Please set me _____ and I'll grant your wish;
A kingdom of wisdom? A palace of gold?
Or all the fancies _____ mind can hold?"
And I said, "Okay," and I set him free,
But he laughed at me as he _____ away,
And left me whispering my _____
Into a silent sea.

Today I caught that fish _____
(That lovely silver prince of fishes),
And once again _____ offered me,
If I would only _____ him free,
Any one of a number of wishes
If I would _____ him back to the fishes.

He was delicious!

1   Write the missing words in the poem.

    | swam fish he set me throw your wish again free |

Answer these questions in sentences.

2   What was unusual about the silver fish?

    _____

3   What did the fish promise his captor?

    _____

4   Do you think the fish was able to grant wishes? Explain your answer.

    _____

5   What happened to the fish in the end?

    _____

Giving directions

The arrow shows where two men are standing. One man is asking the other man for directions. The answers are given below. Write down what the questions were.

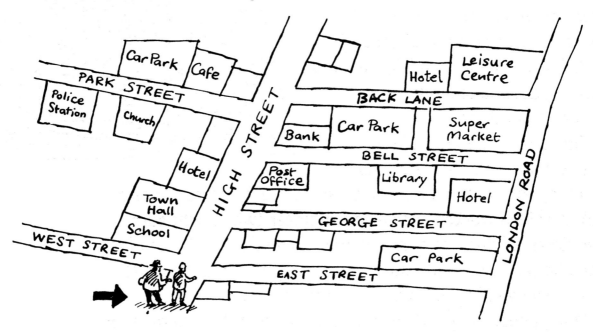

1   "There are three. There is one in Park Street, another between Bell Street and Back Lane. The third one is free and is in East Street."

_____

2   "It is on the corner of High Street and Bell Street. Go up the road and you will see it on your right."

_____

3   "You will find it in Park Street just past the church on the left."

_____

4   "There is the Crown in the High Street, The Ship in Back Lane and The George on the corner of George Street and London Road. Try the Crown, it is the largest, and has the most rooms."

_____

5   "Go along the High Street and take the third turn on your right. You will find it half way down the road on your right."

_____

Diet in Victorian times

Except for the very poor, people's diets began
to include more nutritious foods after 1870.
The importation of refrigerated meat from
Argentina and Australia meant that
more meat was eaten, and cheap fruit
and fish became more widely available.
However, the staple foods were still
bread and potatoes.

   The family of a low-paid man,
such as a farm-worker, had to exist
on bread, potatoes and tea, with meat or eggs perhaps once a
week. A skilled worker, such as an engineer (who might earn
three times as much as a farm-worker), could afford to feed his
family better. They might have meat every day, and their diet
would also include fruit, pastries, coffee and jam.

   Many people suffered illnesses caused either by bad food, or
lack of food. One of the reasons that people today are generally
taller, stronger and healthier than they were a hundred years
ago is that they have a better, more balanced diet.   by Laura Wilson

Answer these questions in sentences.

1   Why was it only the very poor whose diet did not improve after 1870?

   _____

2   What made it possible to import meat from other countries?

   _____

3   What do you think is meant by staple foods?

   _____

4   What effect has a better diet had on people today?

   _____

5   Why would the lack of food and bad food cause people to be ill?

   _____

Name _____ Date _____

The bungalow

1   Read the story carefully. Draw a plan of the grandparents'
    bungalow. Give your plan a title and label each of the rooms.

Sally loved going to stay with
her grandparents. They lived
in a small bungalow not far
from the sea.

    As Sally went in through
the front door and into the
hall, her grandparents'
bedroom was on the right.
Opposite their bedroom was the
sitting room. Further down the hall
and next to the sitting room was a big kitchen.
It was the biggest room in the house. It had a dining area
in one corner where Sally's grandparents had their meals.
The bathroom was on the other side of the hall from the
kitchen. The little bedroom Sally slept in when she visited
her grandparents was between the kitchen and the bathroom
at the back of the bungalow.

2   Turn over and draw a plan of your bedroom. Write a description of it.